MW01598843

LOOKING
WITHIN

WRITTEN AND ILLUSTRATED BY
ARLENE GRASTON

Text and images copyright © 2018 by Arlene Graston
All Rights Reserved

No part of this book may be reproduced, used, or stored in any
information retrieval system or transmitted in any form or by any
means, electronic, mechanical, photocopying, recording, or otherwise,
without prior written permission from the author, except in the
case of brief quotations embodied in critical articles and reviews.
For permission please visit: arlenegraston.com

Book design by Drew Stevens and Arlene Graston

978-0-9848814-8-2 (pbk)
978-0-9848814-9-9 (ebook)

VISIBLES, INC New York

OTHER BOOKS BY ARLENE GRASTON

LET ME REASSURE YOU
Remembering Reality

THE CHILDREN'S PROMISE
A Visit to a Spiritual Garden

DO YOU REMEMBER?
Whispers from a Spiritual World

IN EVERY MOON THERE IS A FACE
Poem by Charles Mathes

THUMBELINA
Tale by Hans Christian Andersen

SPECIAL FRIENDS
Tales of Saints and Animals

Why should not we also enjoy an original relation to the universe? Why should not we have a poetry and philosophy of insight and not of tradition, and a religion by revelation to us, and not the history of theirs?

—RALPH WALDO EMERSON

CONTENTS

WHY I WRITE

✦

IF YOU SAW THE WRITINGS on the walls of my inner room you'd discover the journey my soul and I are making. My heritage is spiritual not human. It is *soft* words that remind me who I am. These words bring me strands of silk that weave themselves through my emotions, giving a kind of sheen to the coarse fabric of my humanness.

In our world an identity forms out of the first remembered awareness of self. For me that was who I was before my physical birth as a human being. I write from the point of view of my eternal nature. I have never stepped out into the world and made myself obvious there. I have never stood in a room full of people and shown my real self. As an artist, I speak in a whisper to celebrate the wonder of life's poetic nature.

This book, then, is not a traditional memoir. I write to keep alive my awareness of what I am that is more than human. How do I know what matters in a world that distorts reality?

I tell myself.

People are whole, why do they act as if they are not? Why have they forgotten about love and their life-giving imagination? Socialized to separate from their inner being as soon as they arrive, most people become total strangers to their own existence. Their time on Earth unfolds to be nothing more than an unconscious search for a self that cannot be found in external things. But the ordinary of life is filled with clues. Within each human "problem" is the truth of reality that can be set free by putting right *our own* perception. The human mind is programmed and shows us a world that imprisons us. We are under a spell. Our real mind is subtle and delicate and thinks along the Current of Life. Let us *be* this subtle mind. Let us be *who we are*.

The material in this book originates from the different perceptual levels of my consciousness and I have arranged each kind of writing into a separate and distinct section. I start with an arrival and end with a story about how I understand the workings of our universe. The book comes together to gently resolve the disparity between the world I live in and what I feel inside.

My book is made of words. My soul inspires from wordless feeling. I hope my book is felt to be more than words. ✧

INTRODUCTION

We used to think that if we knew one,
we knew two, because one and one are two.
We are finding that we must learn
a great deal more about 'and'."
—ARTHUR EDDINGTON
Mathematician, astronomer, physicist

WHEN I WAS FIRST introduced to the world of numbers and
the ways of arithmetic as a little girl in school, I entered a
world I could never befriend. At that very first lesson, when I
was told one and one are two, I innocently asked,

> "But what about the . . . *and*?"

It was an instinctive and emotional question, and I do not
have a sense memory of what prompted me to ask it. But
the answer I got left me worried forever after—to this day I
can't confidently make change or calculate a tip. Apparently,
I had to have an impersonal connection with remote, aloof
symbols and remain outside their feeling world—a world I
knew had to be just like mine, since everything was. Now
I was expected to quantify a reality I couldn't *feel*. Where

had the warm livingness gone? Having to look outside myself I became confused rather than enlightened. I just didn't perceive an impersonal world. I did not know how to interact with one.

What was this intelligence that did not look to itself for answers? *I must put away what I know*, I told myself. *I must think what is not true.* It became difficult to move of my own free will. Hadn't it all been otherwise, just an instant ago?

And so, I, a radiant unlimited being who was now in a limited world, needed codes and markings to communicate with the world around me. Yet for a long time I remained confident and excited to start, itching to get going, jumping for joy to create a happy world I would fill with beauty. I had come here to join with the infinite substance in a new and generous way by taking material clay and making magic with it.

I glowed from a light so bright it lit a path before me waiting to be filled with what I knew was in me. I saw no impediments, material or otherwise, to my life unfolding in perfect freedom. Though in a body I was unfettered, undaunted by time and space and gravity, and for quite a while it remained a world without walls. My mind knew only what was true—I believed in myself and never doubted. It was so wonderful to be alive, to be *me*.

My mind produces my objectified world—the inner creates the outer. I exist from a great love forever expressing. It is my nature to love and to love myself. I can be influenced not to, but only when I no longer know myself.

Our materialistic society presents life as a separated reality I have to be instructed how to fit into. This takes away my autonomy and carefree nature and makes me doubt myself. Now, as I stand in a world with walls, I am too full of artificial thinking to hear my original nature's clarity. I am full to overflowing with philosophies and theologies in frozen imagery; full with science and psychology with narrowing definitions. Life, confined to intellectualized worlds, feels withheld from me and I find myself isolated from the subtle touchpoint to this world that is my body—it is tied into knots.

I feel trapped in those knots. I carry my life as a burden. I drag wishes and wantings up the day's incline. Life feels hard. I am distracted by the hands I have on Sundays that are not the hands I have the rest of the week. But I have no hands, and there are no Sundays. I am simply looking away from my inner peace. I know my integrity is not found caring about hands and Sundays. My integrity is found in just being myself.

Myself is what life is in its simplest, purist terms. My gaze inward shows my outer world's secret: there are diamonds growing in my turnip patch. When I take the quiet inner path, I reconcile its landscape to the illusion I'm seeing and discover the truth about my human life.

I paint. I write. My dialogue with my inner self illuminates the room where I sit and create. I wrap myself in the deeply warm affection from my inner light. I am the recipient of an immensity that becomes my world. I contain, unwoven, all that I will ever be, so I trust what is not yet here. It will come I know.

My word-thoughts are in truth subtle energies. I use simple words to speak of the world my heart knows so well and to write a book about our compassionate nature. I am propelled by my desire to inspire the *feeling* of this noble thing we are. In the feeling is the presence. Life's tenderness is deceptive, it is really power. Unusually lovely things occur in our human existence when contemplating this tenderness.

Since I don't write about a separated reality, my meaning will be heard as the sway of the meadow grasses when there is a *lull in the wind*. That stillness reveals its secrets to childlike hearts and intellects at rest. This book is for basking in gentleness, nothing more. Nothing more is needed. ✧

A LITTLE GIRL AND HER SOUL

A True Story

✦

HOW LONG HAS SEEMED this journey into a dream that had me hiding from myself, pretending to be human. Don't you know how I have wanted to say true things? Don't you know how I have wanted to express the real and everlasting and share it with the rest of life around me? Don't you know?

I came with a light in my pocket. It held reality in trust. It stayed in my pocket, and became a glorious but impotent thing—I felt compelled to agree with this world, wasn't that the point in coming to a place like this? When I did, I became invisible and lost sight of my light. But not my pocket. The others all have a light in their pocket—though they don't even know about the pocket.

I saw only lines out there. I had to stay within the lines. I saw structure from walls and ceilings, boundedness within gates and doors. I became cemented in a cluster of humanity and could not come and go at my own pace or pleasure. That is what I understood when looking outside myself. But the night became softer when I began to speak truthfully of my origins.

My soul is deciphering my human journey. I am learning from its wisdom. My soul is the substance of the earthly gardens I have known and companion to the silent, rooted trees. I have never been truly friendless on this

earth because the light is shared. Its presence glows
in me when I close my eyes and I hear it when I watch
my breath become more than we both remembered
it can be.

My soul tells me I lived the story of a little girl. A little
girl, who in the instant of a wayward thought, lost her
eternalness. She discovered sorrow. Hers is the story of a
light that went out and was replaced by street lamps. Her
gentle mind, once knowing only peace, carried a wounded
hope upon a path that wasn't going anywhere. And yet, all
the while, a luminous shadow hovered. A great love was
present and a pocket held promises.

This tale, often repeated, is of a child who ventured into a
narrative untrue but believed to be true. This is a kind child,
as all children are kind and given to bring the best and the
highest of themselves, if they be allowed to do so.

✦

I am a soul, she said, she as she stood before the reflection
in a mirror and saw only a human. *I am a soul but show it
not.* She cried over this, wanting to be home where what
mattered lived and she mattered, too.

I am a soul, she kept whispering holding aloft the light the
infinite had given her to keep as she descended the stairs to
the darkened room on the spinning ball. She was not afraid
of dark rooms, she knew nothing of stairs. But the light held

a glow that she knew well, and a warmth that made her glad. She longed to be glad more often than she was glad now. Something in her was made for gladness because there was only gladness—a gladness that was truer than the word it had become.

I will not lose sight of the truth, she said as she entered the dream. She knew about the dream. In her deeper self she had been to Time before. It was a difficult place with an agenda of its own, but its perspective was illusory and one had to tread softly through the maze of sleepwalkers. They could not be dealt with harshly and with too much truth. It was interesting how the truth annoyed them. No, it was best to tread most cautiously and keep her knowing silent. *I will not lose sight of the truth,* she promised herself.

But she did.

She was a soul made of freedom but now so many other qualities were attached to her and she attached more to herself, too. Trinkets and charms glittered and tossed themselves about in the movement of her walk down the streets where she lived with her attachments. She was busy that way, keeping the attachments close, grooming them, feeding them, keeping them shiny and sleek that the neighbors would approve. This approval was paramount to her happiness and to her safety. At least she thought this and was committed to this idea.

So the years built upon themselves. Each one made life feel more dense, illusion more real. Where was the vibrancy that stirred her being and made her willing and eager? Where was the bird that lived without a cage and brought her sand roses from faraway places that were just next door? She had been so happy in her little room without walls or a ceiling. A room that did not hold memories but was full of the keepsakes brought from happy thoughts. She missed the friendships of the tender kind, the fulfilled kind. There was never sorrow in the room with no walls or ceiling. There was love and that love was never ever talked about. It was never even thought about. How could it be? It was being expressed. It was giving itself. It was the love in her and in all the treasured keepsakes in her world. It was reality, close and warm.

Inevitably, she grew tired and disheartened carrying the things she had become attached to. Life was heavy and empty. She was no longer simply be-ing. She clearly saw that. Did she?

She was a soul. Wasn't she? Was she? But what was a soul? Could she ask? Whom could she ask? Would she find an answer out there? From anyone? This seemed doubtful. Those whom she could ask were similarly burdened but acted as if they were not.

The way things look is not the way things are. The maintaining of a facade caused her much pain. And eventually the pain brought her wisdom. And the wisdom brought defiance.

I have been mistaken, she said one day. *I have taken a ride to the wrong conclusion. I was not meant to agree!*

I rush around, I grasp and bargain. I judge. I condemn the thing I am from not seeing who I am. It was my true self that stood before me in that mirror. And it was a mirror made for distortion. It is my own self that needs my love and absolution. When I give it, all the troubled thoughts will spin smoothly on an axis built from joy and innocence.

I will go where the air is pure and devoid of dreaming what is not true. No disguise can alter my understanding of the life I am.

And so, she returned herself to Emptiness—whole, complete, emptiness. She went deeply into herself and altered her human existence by what she found there. She saw she stood in the eternal beginning. She was expansive beingness. She was free. She had something to give.

She knew she had not lost the home that waited for her while she resolved a dream that was unlike her nature. She placed her fingers on little keys and wrote of her Heart's infinity. She wrote of the love before birth and the love that waits and the love that accompanies each step through the rooms of a human house.

She is grateful for the reality that is the golden light that opens onto a garden never far away but right here where happiness lives. And she is grateful for her true love and how beloved she is.

✦

This is her story. True in every detail. It is mine, too. We share a soul. ✧

CARVINGS IN THE WINTER SNOW

Entering a Dream

THERE IS NO WAITING . . . IT IS HERE

✦

BE QUIET AND OPEN THE DOOR to Evermore. Be quiet and let all of Life rush in and take its place in consciousness. How different it is to be open to the thing invisible and silent, than it is to be open to the outer world with all its convictions about nothing.

How good it is to *receive* what is from within. A burden of such immense magnitude is lifted. Life becomes what can be expressed with ease. A dear nearness brings joyful exhilaration in being alive. Gone are the other voices. Here is the only Voice flowing through everything, filling the lost places, unraveling oblivion. No more hiding. ✧

MY SECRET PRAYER

✦

IT WAS AT THE START of my story that the oddest thing about it happened. There appeared to be a birth . . . an entrance into reality from no reality. I had to lie about my origins. This lie caused a rift between my soul and me that wasn't there before; one that remained with us in such a peculiar way and for much of a human life. Together we had never known beginnings and endings. Or even partings — never conceived of such things. My soul had always been just me *but now was the one I searched for. I felt only an absence within. For the first time I knew despair. Before that abrupt separation I was timeless, a Self, uninterrupted by otherness.*

What had always been present became unknown to me. I was lonely and sad. I thought my inner being could no longer hear me so I mourned the loss of it. How empty I was not to have the one who listened, who cared, who kept me safe. I lost my beloved Heart.

And now, by the light of my resolve, I reach for my dearest soul in the depth of my enchanted sleep. I am finding it wholly with me. To make it real to my mind blesses my objectified world with more than passing fancies. I make it real again to my mind and regain my beloved Heart. ✧

HEART MURMUR

✦

I WANT TO CRY for the times I have thought myself alone
and far from meaning. I want to cry for thinking myself
so wrong that I have to live someone else's truth and
not my own.

I want to cry for thinking the Eternal is banning me from Its
hearth. I want to cry for having thought I had to leave my
sacred garden and believe I am not what I am. I want to cry
for thinking I could not be a truthful person. I want to cry for
thinking that I could lose knowledge of reality and engage in
a falseness of living.

Why, oh, why, would I ever want to go where what is said
is untrue? Why does such a place exist? But does it exist as
I perceive it?

I think and find brambles at my feet made from worries as
the path before me becomes obscured by my darkened
view. I tread with uncertainty and head for the distant hills
hoping that the way will open before fear takes hold of me
and moves me in the wrong direction. There is only a hint
of moon now showing through the forest that has sprung
around me from the thoughts in my mind. Branches move
their leaves in a slow lament.

And yet, and yet, look carefully, there is a small clearing in
the night that opens onto daylight allowing the saddened

soul to see and be assured. There is on the horizon a little bit of sun left over from a hopefulness believed in long ago. Yes there is hope in the air; everywhere.

I am walking and wondering what purpose this journey is based on. The commands are loud and intrusive and the sound coming from the grief in others makes the peace and quiet that comes from within hard to hear. How does one turn away and listen to the nothing? How does one do that? There must be a way to stay peaceful where peace is not believed in. There must be a way to view the origin of life through the brittle illusion of time. I am at a loss to understand this dream.

Thankfully, I am only a dreamer destined to wake up. I will not despair; there must be a purpose to this darkness. I know that light lives in the recesses hidden from my view.

I must be going through this jungle of thoughts . . . to bring the truth to my thinking. ✧

THE HAMSTER LOVES HIS WHEEL

✦

AS I DESCEND THE STAIRS to enter Time each morning, I know that the sun will be revolving in and out of my awareness—I see the world through intermittent thoughts. Yet my soul's constancy is not absent even in a dream.

But I've become a dreamer and am confused by the hollow in my heart that once was full beyond imagining. I am now only the friend of a friend of a friend to myself. That is how things are for me in this material world down those stairs. I am that far removed from my dear little self and I am not happy about this. I sometimes regret having taken this journey. Was I aware when I planned it, that the journey would be so circuitous and ruinous to my peace of mind? I don't remember.

It is important that I know why I am having such a contrary experience. And the answer is that I already harbored mental bedlam before I came. At least, a part of me did. In coming here I could resolve what fruitless thought patterns persist in me. To not be in the human dimension doesn't mean that one is free of that dimension. There are interlocking corridors to planes of consciousness where unresolved and limiting beliefs can throw the whole out of whack and keep one stuck.

This to me is nothing more than the hamster's little wheel going round and round, lifetime after lifetime. Ironically, it is all the result of belief. Still, it requires an act of courage to get off that wheel.

Awareness while in the dream sets me free from my own habitual little cycle. It is freedom I'm after, not endless lifetimes in misperception because I already know something massively wonderful: *there is a beauty in me that wants to be expressed; a light from which I see infinity; a goodness that makes me sing while its presence in me fills me with unspeakable joy.*

It is true, I often have fun in this land of make-believe despite its challenging ways. I know it is possible to fill my time here with the Light, the Goodness and the Love that are the qualities of the only life there is. But I have to let go of the thoughts causing strife. The only mistakes I ever make are when I choose human purpose rather than Soul purpose. (Of course, this with a bit of coercion from the world, let's be fair.)

There is only one Mind and my mind is an activity of its consciousness. The greater Mind doesn't make mistakes or need to accrue endless lifetimes of lessons. Knowing I am that Mind is the answer to all my questions. I am meant only to live from my true identity.

What I want most of all in life, is to hear the Silence. Softly breathing in hiddenness, this silence is what I am and where I come from. It is life's wholeness, and mine. And though I play at being something else, something answerable to other people, obligated to more than the Silence, I've kept my Self—only a part of my awareness is focused as a human being. I wear her face. She hears me in her heartbeat and only a few small attitudes have been impeding her ease of life.

In humanness is a heart that doesn't pretend; its beat sounds what is true. It is Joy that is found in that heart and brings to experience more than a fleeting whirl of days and nights. Wisdom stands by patiently with hand outstretched to guide the human to the joyful source within. Every human has a heart pulsing with this joyful presence waiting to be known.

When I became a human I chose to remember it was a dream I was dreaming and remain conscious within it. This is my act of courage. ✧

THE MOON THAT TIPS HIS HAT

✦

I WONDER ABOUT THE MOUNTAIN as it towers tall and regal. I wonder what it thinks as it surveys the scene below where I live. Above us the moon politely tips his hat when he reappears amid the stars that twinkle at midnight. I wonder about him, too.

I wonder and wonder about the little man who lives alone on the edge of the village in the house just like mine. He says nothing but looks to be of good disposition. A good disposition is what I seek. I think it would make me happy to have one. I do not have one now but I did, once. I'm not sure how I lost it.

I know that it fills all of creation, this thing called happiness, but where I live in the shadow of that tall mountain, there is darkness of spirit. There are beliefs growing deep underground that have caused the people of this valley to fall asleep and dream of a world of their own perceiving.

Imagination here is underground, too. The people sleep to keep from feeling happy. Happiness is the thing they fear the most, for it surely must come with a price. It can't be the thing that permeates the air they breathe, the warmth that ripples over the skin they think they're in and what will bolster their will with purpose when they need it to.

A great Light is invisible to them though it is their own light vibrating cells that become mountains, a moon and twinkling stars within a singing universe. Even in the darkest corners of the valley there are warm gentle nights when tiny sparkles of light can be seen but the people say they are only fireflies. Bugs. The children trap them in jars.

Imagine.

I remember now, it was on hearing this kind of thing one too many times that I gave up my happy disposition. It was just too much work to remain contrary to such conviction. I know I shouldn't have done that. I only ended up disappointing myself and disappointment in self dims the truth in everything you look at. I see only fireflies, too.

Oh, I become so very unhappy, when I let other people influence me away from what I know. ✧

THE PIPER FROM THE HILLS ABOVE

✦

YES, I FORGOT I AM THE RIVER that carries Life's electric matter through countless worlds. In my human dream I sit only on its banks listening to the Piper from the Hills Above. His music soothes my brow with the warmth of the Eternal and I almost hear the vows that were made as I fell asleep to my nature.

I have been standing in a mind full of enchanting threads that unraveled me from myself. They are absorbing and intriguing with their enticing ways. I followed them to find myself not mistress of my own wanting. They removed my quietness to engage me in an outer reality that handed me deception.

Before the dream I knew my Self full well. My inner sky was rich with stars becoming brilliant plums for eating. This sky was my life-giving orchard. Now, only memories fill my nights and days. My humanity is made of thoughts about a past and future—where has the *present* gone?

Thankfully, the Piper's tune echoes my own heart's beat where the truth is known. Receiving it, I will *be* the present. ✧

SO CLOSE IS WHAT MATTERS

A Mystical Humanity

IT ALL GOES AWAY

✦

I HEAR LITTLE PEALS OF LAUGHTER in the petals of the flowers. I see sparkling drops of dew. The morning shines all over me as if the day's beginning were a thing to embrace. I no longer wander the maze of my yesterdays.

Nothing in me, nothing that is mine, is harmed by the mistakes I have allowed to be made by my idle and fruitless human mind and its forgetting. I have discovered, to my utter relief and delight, that making a mistake is a reminder to *let go*. It brings the understanding that dissolves all regrets, remorse, and punishment. Letting go is the Blessing my self-awareness brings when I am not believing all the things I've been *told* by a world lost in obscurity.

Now I can hear the laughter in the petals of the flowers. And I learn the sparkling drops of dew are my tears of rejoicing that what is true about me will always be true about me, even while I live in this world that tells me otherwise. ✧

THISTLEDOWN

✦

IN A SOFT SECLUDED PLACE within me I see without eyes but have true vision.

In its soft warm nest rests my heart, holding forever the keys to every mystery.

In the soft curve of time that is a day, a light burns that never dims.

The world I come from seems unreal to a world made of make-believe. Something very soft brings me to aliveness. Something that is no more than a thought.

It's just a glance away, this inner world of mine where peace and perfection live. Its presence before me needs nothing but my smallest thought about it. I gently touch its hem and it becomes my world.

Simple is the way to the eternal reality. I am what I want to know before I ask. Here within me is the warm reassuring blush of a deeper world. I see order in the midst of chaos. I let that chaos be as nothing because it is only my attention upon it that gives it life. To spurn it makes it fly away.

I do not come from a mother's body, I am from the everlasting. I have the countenance given to me by the one breath. I have the companions formed by the one heart. Tucked within the human day is my eternal home. I have nothing other than what I am. ✧

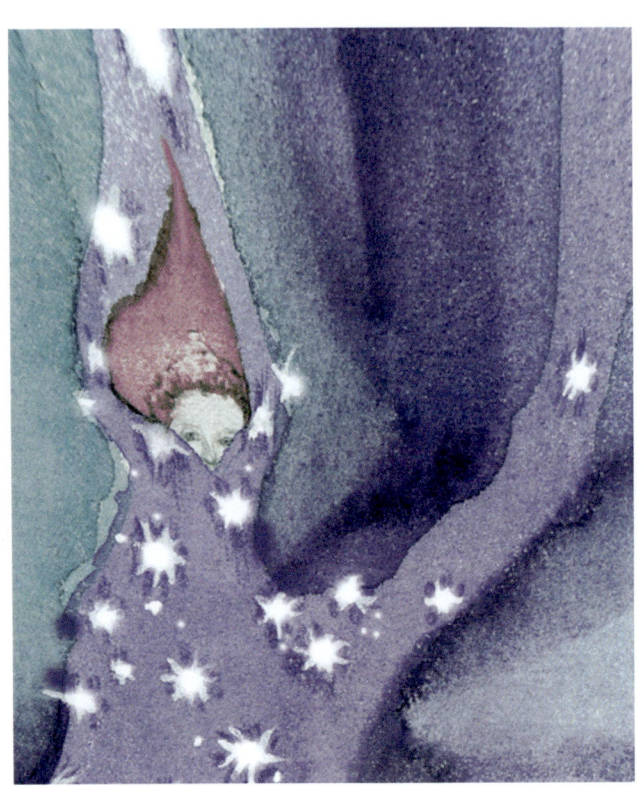

THE PRESENCE IN THE EMPTY ROOM

✦

WHEN I AM HOME in heaven I have an empty room. It is a place of calm and creativity in a deep feeling light that holds me near and dear. Emptiness is not a vacuum, you know. Within it is Everything.

On Earth, I am not often in an empty room and this is a problem. So many objects seek my attention, both animate and otherwise. In empty rooms there is so very much space—so much room to imagine. Imagine what can be imagined in a quiet place to contemplate eternity. Imagine *oh yes, we all know* what can be created in such stillness.

" Oh, I just love that empty room of mine and I love what it does to my outlook. I hear my heart and my heart shows me all the delights in being alive. It is so very nice there. I don't know why it cannot be known on Earth. ✧ *"* *~ perhaps it can in some way: indeed you have described it.*

43

LOVE TALK

✦

SCIENCE BE DAMNED—it is Love that brings up the morning sun. The world is my inner self. They tell me this isn't true, but I don't listen to them. After all, I am not standing here empty, alone and unaided—I am alive. My aliveness creates.

My mind is intelligence. Its effortless ways may be hidden from me but when I reach within I find what I am looking for. I need nothing from the outer world of many pictures, my identity is the everlasting, it brings what is needed to form my wholeness.

So well I know this today

Feb. 2, 2019 – an experience "R/b/G " never to be forgotten

A saw:

Being possessed of a magical soul, I am meant to see a landscape formed by deep sweeping harmonies. I soar when I think the morning's shining droplets are created by me. How reassured is my small mind when I don't think that a world in pain is the real one. The unhappy world I see makes me bring the Light to my awareness. That is the power I possess. The only reason for seeing loss is to remind myself reality is standing where I am.

Kind of twinnie my

I am Imagination. I am the artist who brushes the sky in colors newly born each moment. I am loved and loving. Adored and adoring. I am Happiness's Child. I have only my heart to offer the world. ✧

i would love to see A to give her just one more

44

THE SECRET IN THE PLAIN AND SIMPLE

✦

THE UNIVERSE LONGS TO SHOW ITSELF. It will not reveal its mystery to me until I move into expression. That is why faith was invented. I do not know what lives in me until my act of faith.

All is consciousness. All. A little earthenware jug that is empty now, *believes* in itself and knows that it will hold thick rich cream. Or flowers. Silent objects sitting on the sideboard of my life have worthwhile things to tell. They have been created to express fulfillment. There is hidden in the ordinary a greater scheme waiting to be understood. Divinity comes in the guise of plain and simple symbols gamboling through my world. A jug is not *just* a jug.　*So true —*

I give myself over to this playful life that erupts in the air around me. I join in without a plan, without a map, without a doubt. A great love is waiting to reveal itself to me as I dance about—the love that I have for being alive.

The world is waiting, too. It needs my uniqueness to be a complete picture. That's the assurance that was made to me when I embarked on this journey. ✧

I KNOW A BIRD

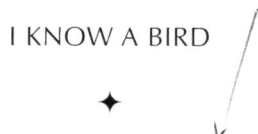

WHAT DO YOU WANT? asked the bird sitting on the branch of my tree. It sang its words and I realized that I was entering a lovely day.

What *do* I want? I asked myself.

I want to know what the wind is saying. I want to know the secret the bells are revealing in their chime. I want to know how the sun makes its rounds in the world when its origin is the center of my heart. I want to know all the wonders of life in this world and any other. "

maybe
for
Karen
Katie

But what I truly want, is to freely be myself in a world that pulls me outward to obey what is not true.

Oh Yes! said the bird. Be that. ✧

" I day after such a long time,

A - the Knowledgeable, wondering. —
perfect contemplative!

THE OTHER ME

✦

DON'T BE SAD, said the sun to the cloud filling up with tears. But the rain fell anyway. Then the night arrived and the day went away.

Where did it go? Where had it come from? Time is passing, but where to? Where am I now? These are the questions I ask.

No, no, no, you may not use my book for your silly questions. I need order. I am collecting stardust. It is everywhere but must be enticed from the breezes. That's why I stand apart, free of loud silly questions and let the subtlety gather round me—it is drawn magnetically to what is perfectly *still*. Then it will fill my pockets; settle on my hair and into the holes made by my forgetting. I will sparkle from within. I will be what once I was. And then, I'll remember all kinds of things beyond belief. I'll even have the answers for all your silly questions.

That's me, a dreamer gathering stardust. You pass me by while I go looking for the marvelous you don't believe in. You believe in questions. We scarcely ever meet.

One day, I put my Great Wish in a pot and it grew a flower; a flower that sprouted new life beneath the protective scab of my old despair. It is all explained, she said, in the Book that is not a book in your House that is not a house. Read it. Trust it. Rely on it.

I did. I do. I am. In it I read about my home in heaven because I am not really from Earth. I come from where things do not go away. I don't know why or where they go to in this world where they do go away all the time.

This world is odd in many ways. I will have to figure this thing out, or just not care and I don't think I have to care. I'm only dreaming about wondering about things like this. Asking a lot of questions hasn't gotten me anywhere. *Being perfectly still* is what has moved me to write this book of mine that you are reading and fill it with words and pictures from my heaven. ✧

"iT is the secret "

WHAT I AM

✦

I FIND MY NAME in the vastness showing me the path of least resistance. There is a road before me and all it does is open to what is mine and takes me to what belongs to me.

so lovely

I am the wind. I am the song the moon sings to itself in the morning when its face pales in the new sunny sky. I am the rain that makes beauty and delight on my windowpane and I am the fire that glowed all through the night to warm the winter's breath. I am the root of the tree that fills the world with its reminders of a caring constancy.

The I AMS

I am on a remarkable human adventure. I hear the silent roar of the great Being and I wonder how the sleepers of this planet can be so willing to lose sight of the wonderfulness *they* are. ✧

✦

ETERNITY IS NO FARTHER AWAY than my willingness to know who I am. I know Life very personally. It knows me. We are in love. We perceive one another. I am endowed with pure perception. I am the innocent onlooker, knowing truthfully. I don't see what others see. Others don't see what I see. We all see truly.

It is a very great honor to play at being a person and it is so simple a thing to be the person I am. I need not take myself to the mountain top to feel Infinity's presence, it indwells me more deeply than does the breath that moves my body.

So close is the Thing that matters. So simple is the way to it. It is uncomplicated and immediate. It is here and now in the midst of the perceived chaos of human living. I bless that chaos and call it by its rightful name: *forgetfulness.* The outer picture had me confused as I sought approval from a world that does not know itself. The chaos was in me fighting the world. I bring myself to peace in finding who I am. When I look within, all that confused me vanishes. Perception is my power. My happiness is found in my true perception. My being is honorable and I am wise in my use of perception. Reality is my clear thought and pure awareness. Truth is steadfast within me. ✧

THEY THINK I'M SHY

✦

I WALKED TO THE EDGE of my world again this morning and let in the day. It brings itself to me after a round of moon to sun. I expect it to do this, so I just quietly watch it reappear.

My life on Earth is designed to stay within neat little boxes and I move around in them obediently. I can do only so much within each one, just as I can walk only so far in any distance. I had to learn to understand and to obey these definitions; they were new to me once. Now, I work within them mostly well and pretty wisely. Not everybody does.

Today came to me like all the other days—new and fresh _" I belong to the morning "_ and seemingly pleased to bring itself. I saw it had no hesitation. I, too, had none. I've grown quite accustomed to this regimented way of doing things. I've become familiar with this reliably reoccurring world and go about its expanses collecting odd bits of stuff and trivia to bolster my sense of self. In my room are shelves that never seem to mind another thing to hold. That is how I live now. And what I do.

I am comfortable with the inanimate objects of my world, but it is the people I find truly puzzling. So I don't speak much. Why should I? They don't seem to understand why I care more about an invisible reality than I do a visible one. ✧

TO FIND WHAT IS NOT LOST

✦

FLIGHTS INTO UNHAPPINESS do not tell me who I am. The world around me does not tell me who I am. Where do I go for the truth? This ardent search has replaced life's reassuring simplicity.

Every day I push the river. I am so tired but I applaud my willingness to toil like this. Endeavor rather than ease is in my bones. I persevere and call myself brave though I am the source of all my misery. What I am is a creator. What I need is faith.

I will sit here now and bring my attention to the moment at hand. There is no other moment, no other time, no other place but this. This instant holds me in a tenderness I'd forgotten could exist. I surrender, and the great love that warms the center of my being engulfs me in freedom. I am free from history, free from personality, free from judgment. But I am real.

I do not find myself in the sounds and sights that make my world. Though I am the creator of that world, the giver of all I experience, I cannot see myself out there—*I am not made of fleetingness.* ✧

KINDRED SPIRIT

✦

I SAT AT A WINDOW the other day that looked upon a scene of such wonder that my heart was heard to speak. No human words came but truths were uttered. In the moment of hearing these whispers and knowing their meaning, I was healed of a deep and long-standing sorrow.

I have nothing to say, sighed the bird on my window sill. It sat there all day too, just looking at the trees in the park as their leaves turned to russet and gold. I understood. It was touched by all that Beauty and there was nothing to say about it. The moment was Full and we were fulfilled.

Apparently birds know what matters. ✧

✦

I AM UNCONCERNED with the ending of my human existence. My life had no beginning to bring to an end. I have gone nowhere and I have acquired nothing I can lose or leave behind. I merely *imagined* myself inventing and playacting. I wore a mask and used a language made of sound. And when I will have had enough, I will simply open my true eyes and see I am not standing in a dream anymore.

Wherever I am in the spaciousness of the mind I am made of, reality will never be found outside of my self. What I tell myself is important; I do not limit my words to the definitions I hear in a world thought to be material. I keep telling myself the truth—that is the only little rule I cannot forget to obey.

No, there is no loss when leaving this dream, for all I loved there is still with me. All I ever love is always with me—my heart is where love originates and I am never without my heart. I only have a problem when I take unreal things too seriously. ✧

(handwritten margin notes: "Great for the card!", "Memory", "The only rule", "✳", "Facing the reality at its best")

THE BENEVOLENT LAW

✦

I LIVE UNDER THE WING of the One. Warmly sheltered, I expand and grow and create.

I barely notice the troubles believed out there. They are created by those choosing to expand and grow and create in a manner different from mine. We are all free.

Daily I make my choice: I imagine myself under the wing of the One, and the love I meet up with is the Love that fills my heart and my daily needs as I remain sheltered in reality. ✧

ONLY HUMAN

✦

THERE ARE TIMES IN THE DAY when I feel so out of touch with reality. I place myself in limbo and tell myself what a shame that I don't know how to fill this moment. But why do I feel so impotent? Why do I feel inadequate?

It is an interesting thing this inadequacy. Perhaps, it is a truth. Perhaps, I *am* inadequate. Perhaps I am telling myself a truth and should be listening. As a human I have nothing to offer myself or the world around me. As a human I playact a temporary role; I deal only in borrowed knowledge. As a human I only use the *coins* of the realm, which are all finite. When I believe I am only human, I limit myself.

But I am not only human. I am the face and fingers of the One. And when I let myself be that, I don't even think about being inadequate—or adequate. ✧

A VERY WARM BLANKET

✦

LOOK, IT IS SNOWING! How soft and quiet the day becomes as the whiteness covers the Earth in a warmth that belies the cold I have been told it brings. My life became crowded looking to an outer world and giving it so much attention. So much, I tell you, nothing was left for me.

And now the snow without uttering a word is erasing trees and the hum of the people around them. As I watch I know the trees love this moment. They are embraced in the sound they and I look forward to each year—the *hush* of our translucence.

The dormant leaves deep within the frozen limbs are rejoicing at this moment, too. They wait within a sleeping breath for their call to awaken from slumber. They are gathering strength even as they remain curled and nestled in invisibility. That which will be the future has begun its life from within the depths of nothingness where all true things find origin. Just as I in each moment that opens itself find myself coming forth to reveal I am much much more than the 'splendor of being human.' I rejoice in what I am.

Oh, I do love to sit like this and write down what is true—I'll relive it in my shadowed moments. It is well I have myself to go to when I want to speak of real things. ✧

SEEING CLEARLY

✦

THE TINY FLOWER ON YOUR LAPEL is very pretty. It has a beauty I find enchanting. There are colors bordering its petals that constantly change and shift and the mood of the room changes with them.

I am happy to see this flower on your dress. It has opened my eyes to a world that I could not envision before; or even believe with my everyday mind. At first I thought myself a victim of misperception. But I do know that a deeper reality is occurring in the course of a day and that *many* royal adventures have not been ventured upon due to not *believing* in the possibilities. Thankfully, today, I believe.

I see that you have been carefully listening to me and that you are noticing the little a crescent moon pulsing in each of my buttons. It is a gift from your flower. Thank you.

Ah, it's a wonderful reality, this one. ✧

cf. p.68 --
make a series of
the moons.

QUILTS COME FROM HEAVEN

✦

THE EARTH IS ENVELOPED IN LOVE—the Invisible becomes visible in gentlenesses.

I see this wonder in Quilts. What human-made artifact has more love and practicality poured into its minutest bit of self? What has ever been created more humbly, more modestly, more patiently, more generously, more simply . . . only to end up more beautifully? These qualities, Virtues all, speak only to the Sublime. And in my world, the Sublime is a quiet thing, a simple thing, a useful thing that honors the body and soul of human life.

I admire anyone who has sewn a coverlet like this. I bless all the unknown women (and men) who have made them and never told us who they were. I, myself, have never sewn a quilt and probably never will. And yet, and yet . . . in the mysterious ways of these things, it was brought to my awareness that, in a way, I *do* make quilts. There is wonder waiting for us in Art. Like prayer, it has the ability to help us see more than what we thought was there. I don't use a needle and thread in my "quilts," I use paint and a very tiny brush. And I use my *heart*; a lot of heart—the essential ingredient for any work of art. ↖

The Universe is ALIVE to me—*each single moment of it.* Each seemingly empty space vibrates from within me and touches my mind with a meaningful Presence. When I paint I show this aliveness. My skies are not flat, my flowers are not just made from petals—they show the stars. I fill up sheets of paper with lots of little squares, each denoting its measure of life in that particular place I've put it. My art needs *lots and lots* of little squares. And isn't that just what a quilt does, too, with its incalculably tiny stitches, its myriad bits of fabric, all coming together to show a wondrous whole; a joyful joining revealing the oneness of all things.

Quilts are truly something special. Their existence confirms our spiritual nature. And they do this in a most important way: they keep us warm and feeling safe and loved. They uplift us with the beauty that lives in Simplicity. And through the living heritage of generations, they connect us to one another in the present and throughout all of time. We need them now just as much as in days gone by and, thankfully, they are being made, devotedly.

They are a reminder that people are . . . good. ✧

THE PARTING GIFT THAT STAYED

✦

I AM THE POSSESSOR of a gift made from the flowers that left my garden for their new home under the Eternal Sun. These flowers are the dearest friends to have for in leaving they bestowed upon me a *Timeless Petal*—one from each.

There were so many that instantly I devised to make a pillow. A nice big round one, filled with remembrance of cherished friends. These Petals have never perished or become dry and brittle. They have remained lovely as ever they were. They fill my room with a scent that enraptures me in restfulness. My quiet times are wonderful.

I speak rarely about this gift, but today it felt right to do so. It's just that kind of book. ✧

THE HOLDER OF MY SECRET

✦

THERE IS A MYSTICAL DISCERNMENT flowing through the branches of the tree outside my window. It is my friend and it patiently waits for me to be aware. The tree is making this human journey with me, to comfort me, to hold the place. All trees have come to hold fast to the subtle world for those fast asleep to their innocence.

I live in a world made of the thoughts accumulated on my passage through Time—they hold me immobile. Though I am encumbered now, I contain the deep goodness that changes my life when I remember the presence of the silent One whose dream adventure this is. I am Its beloved human person. I am visible and invisible, and both all at once. One of us understands this better than does the other.

When I feel I am only the person but allow for wonderment, the outside world rights itself as if by magic. It helps to not heed the world but to be detached from it in warm indifference—then so much that is hard to understand about it becomes less worrisome. Already here is the full measure of life, heard in the stillness the trees affirm. ✧

Stillness

The great little treasure known so very little for what it is, so very rarely appreciated

73

MY REAL FINGERTIPS

✦

HIDDEN IN MY HANDS is a great wonder—a love, a goodness, a *life*, that wants expression. There is within me that which fills my sense of self and moves me to create my world from light and laughter.

I see that the earth and encircling sky are my inventions, too. But I do not dwell on passing pictures. I bask instead in the continuing presence of the internal from which I articulate a world I fill with what I have to give.

I see what appears before me and call it mine, for it is. And on days my worldly canvas displays shadows instead of steady light, I do not despair. That too, is not to be dwelled upon or kept in place with worry. I turn to the invisible that courses through my fingertips; I lean on what lives within me. I believe. I call a loss a blessing that is waiting to reveal it possessed a loving promise all along.

And then . . . I watch it prove me right. ✧

MAGICAL INNERNESS

✦

*I HAD A DREAM ONCE about a strange but charming
world. In it very small thoughts dotted my horizon and I
saw, heard, tasted and touched what was not really there. A
chain of beliefs danced me round and round, arranging and
rearranging the look of the horizon and my mood. I found
myself swept up by what was not from me. Where had I
gone? What was bewitching me?*

✦

So beautiful

Reverently I enter the moment and hang my hat on the peg
near the door that opens into my hidden chamber. I look
inward and reward myself with a fuller picture of my life
and the scenes there reflect my dearest aspirations.

There hangs a basket on another peg. It swings gently in
the wind that whistles through the open window then
sways to the Dance the whistle inspires. This room within
me fills me with sweet Silence. I will bring this peace to
my human life. ✧

*If i could say all day every day only this
how great it would be a "thankyou" to life
as gift*

*this a.m. ɣ = radiance of the
ɣ6—*

as presence

i love this line

76

WHAT IS A SPIRITUAL LIFE?

✦

FREQUENTLY I CALL TO THE WIND and it answers with
a joyful whisper that sets me free. I know I am not alone
in the Earth's busyness. The flowers and trees are my
companions; as are the birds that fly, the insects that crawl,
the desert's sands and the cloud's liquescence that populate
my mornings and nights. These are my fellow travelers under
our sky of blue. I know them all. I feel their kind glowing
faces look back at me and their smiles are meant for me—
we are one.   oh yes! —

My world teems with wonder; I see all the wonder there is.
I am wide awake and sure that the world that surrounds me
is the world that the God of myself is portraying from
Its Infinite Love.

It is people who confuse me. They're the ones who talk
about a spiritual life. All I see there is an ancient tradition
of using rituals to substitute for *self.* ✧

That is all
you see.

That doesn't mean
that is all
that is.

77

IT IS MY NATURE

✦

I DON'T HEAR WORDS as I prepare to write. I thought I
had to hear words announce themselves while I simply
transcribed. But it doesn't work that way. I write within a
mystery waiting to be known.

*p 79 from:
looking
within
Arlene Graston*

*Begin, take a chance, unfurl yourself into the void and be
surprised by what was spellbound a moment ago.*

How daring I must be in this world to trust this thing I am.
I play with the unknown. I feel so humble and small so it
is hard to believe I contain bright promises. And yet, I do.
It is my nature. My nature can walk through unexpected
doorways; make openings in the sky or on the earth;
scamper over high garden walls, and bring the world sweet
secret entrances to Evermore.

Such is the mystery of life that what *is true* cannot be
seen but must be trusted in. And as for what is seen, it is
yesterday's child, let it go.

*yesterday's
child!
let it go!*

Something pours out of me when I let it. All I need do is face
this moment as if there is no other moment before or after,
because there isn't.

No strain, says my heart—the one that brings new ideas and
better ways of doing things. I just need to let my life flow.
That is my nature. ✧

THE BLUE WIND

✦

THERE CAME A STRANGE WIND to my world this morning.
It blew in through the windows sealed shut for generations
and turned my mind into a deep horizon that brought me
back to my senses. I see myself: I am an *untamed* thing.

Divine unruliness should have made me a free being but
I became a good little girl instead. Spiritual wildness is
thought mad by all that is normal. Ha! In a troubled world,
it seems unwise to cheer oneself on from the unchecked
depths of pure Spirit.

Loss of self occurs in the attempt to keep things on an even
keel out there. But today a mystical blue wind came. It
rushed in dispersing the entrancements that held me bound.
Convoluted beliefs are untangled. Life is made plain.

There are stirrings in me now as I write, but what I am really
doing is making myself real in the world. I've been agreeing
with other people's thinking to keep the peace. Now I
embrace my outrageousness.

This is a dangerous thing to do, but I am repossessing the
authentic self I put away. I now have the rich perception I
had before Time shut my eyes with sleep. I see Eternity and
I am in it. My sky is immense. My room has no walls. My
heart is unafraid to love. My life has purpose and meaning.

I am alive.

Yes, alive, but not as it is portrayed by the world. I no longer care what they think as I stand confidently untouched by the Ancient Fears.

The light burning in my inner chamber glows softly, impervious to gusts of worldly tempests. Its warmth brings me only what is my own understanding of the life I am and I find I am utterly charming in my Divine insanity. ✧ ?? // ??

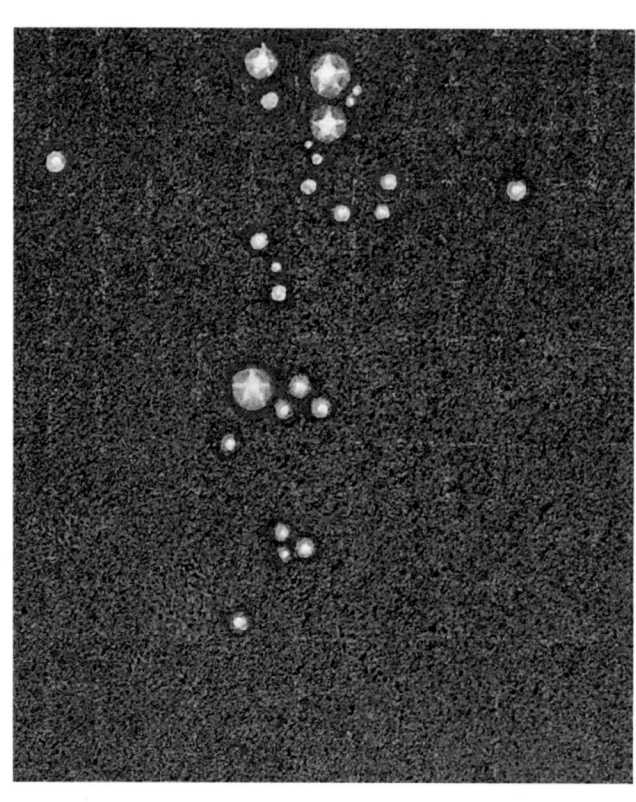

LET GO, IT WHISPERED

✦

A SPARROW COMES TO SIT on my shoulder. I am the branch it clings to. My deepest heart is what it wants to be near. But, alas, my heart hangs from a thread beneath my breast; I cannot even hear it beat.

I am lost, said the sparrow, I cannot find my heart. It, too, has but a thread holding its heart to its breast.

Two stubborn threads are all that connect us to our hearts. I am so near to the sparrow sitting on my shoulder that I hear his unsaid wishes. He leans so close that my thread and his become entwined, twist, and soon break free. Oh!

My heart is no longer hanging from a thread beneath my breast. My heart has been set free. My heart is not captured by weariness and wear, my heart is flying through the air.

There, is my heart, floating on the movement its beating alone makes. There, is my heart, sloping through the strands of time to remain disentangled and freed from disenchantment. I am full now, knowing freedom, holding firmly only to my Self and finding strength in movements unrestricted, unimpaired. Free as a bird is my heart as I soar in the big, bright Wholeness that now is my sky. ✧

THE WALL THAT WASN'T

✦

DO YOU SEE THE GARLAND OF BUTTERFLIES draped around my garden—there, where the horizon touches Heaven? They came when I built the wall. They and I wonder what would cause me to build a wall and close off Heaven.

Nevertheless, sweet thoughts come to me when a butterfly passes by. I hear their peaceful whispers through the vapid ruminations that close me in just like that wall I built.

So I stand and watch the butterflies. My mind follows the tracings of fluttering wings and is moved to simplicity. I let this miracle of thinking nothing fill me. Miracles show themselves when walls of thought do not shut them out.

I now perceive that my garden grows and flowers from my Soul's own gentle soil and sun. The buds on the trees become blooms, the air fills with birdsong. We all stand together in new growth honoring the vastness of the sky where the horizon touches Heaven.

Nothing matters but knowing that the material world is an impressive spell set upon my mind to portray joyful enchantments and charms. It exists to be the setting for my Soul's genius and exuberance. How small is my world when I believe that my genius is of human origin and I limit life to that.

I know little lights will appear above my garden and shine through the night. They hint of the eternal Light that cannot be seen in the separated brightness of the noonday sun. My garden is the painting made by my inner being.

oh how beautiful

✦

When love becomes summer, its warmth persuades the honeysuckle to climb the wall of my garden. My deepest human desires are placed in each flower growing there. I know my dreams will all come true when my faith fills my sky. My garden's fruits and flowers are the fulfillment of my self. I am the sweet earth I stand on. I am the light that makes a summer sun shine.

In viewing my garden from the vantage point of self-acceptance I see full well what I possess. My arms contain a wealth of possibilities with which to create worlds of grace and beauty out of the substance that breathes me into being.

A pattern of goodness lives within me, it contains the living word the Silence speaks. ✧

N.B.!

THE LITTLE BUTTON FROM THE SUN

✦

IT'S HERE! The little button from the sun that wakes me up each day with its cheery chime and I am happy to be alive.

Now tell me true, what could be more wonderful than the work I do? Tell me, tell me, what could be more reassuring? What better way to celebrate this brand new moment than to bring the world good news?

Isn't it exquisite this Wonderfulness that pours out of me? This Fine Feeling I feel from a peaceful mind. This roar of laughter in my heart.

Tell me, tell me do, isn't it wonderful this world I show? This world that comes up like a whisper but blossoms and blooms right before my eyes and says: "Look, here in the corridors of what appears to be a mad world is the secret entryway to your glorious and happy self. You know the way, you have the means and you tell the story."

I see that nothing is missing. I am in need of no one to begin. My self is here, complete and ever ready. I trust. I *make the choice* to trust. Trust enables me. It upholds me and gives me courage. Trust is the little button from the sun that comes to me each morning of my human life to remind me who I am and that I am created to express Joy. Yes, I am. ✧

ANGELS DANCING
ON THE HEAD OF A PIN

When Love Explains

✦

EACH DAY FOR A FEW MINUTES, I write quietly without thought. I let myself be in the Light. Something happens. Things are said. I am spoken to by a voice beyond the hypnotic earthbound dream.

The human view of life is not conscious of the reassuring presence of self within. An incomplete view of life comes at me all day, every day and I lose touch with the only thing I absolutely need to know.

Because Reality has a gentle voice, and the world is insistent and loud, I become entrenched in the world and on some days more than others. I find it harder to believe my inner guidance. Life flows outward from within me. The discipline of writing turns me in the right direction. The world's authority is dispelled and I am no longer alone without myself.

The voice addressing me here is the self I am when I am not the human. There is only *one* being. Ever. ✧

✦

Mornings exist for waking to a dream.

You are asleep to the greatness of being. It is in small batches that comprehension is possible for your human mind. And so you take your life in bits and pieces and call it, "today." In that manageable corner of time and space you become as much of the truth as you can allow.

If in each moment you look inside yourself and say: *What is it, little one, that you have the desire to BE?* Then, the Secret One within you will be known by you and allowed to shine as your world. Honor your deepest self in all ways. ✧

→ RE-VISIT

i think it wants (at least in some way) to be what it was this a.m whole as ③

ANGEL II

✦

I am your True Nature, in spite of all the things you feel about yourself and the world that whirls about you. At the deepest center of your being is peace. It is a peace not known in the world. In fact, the world about you is in your mind, an illusion about yourself.

You want to come to Me and wrap yourself in love and absolute acceptance. Trust in your ability to do this. Trust the subtlety of your mind. Trust. Trust Me. Trust yourself. We are one in peaceful harmony even while there appears a world in uproar.

You wonder how to come to Me and live from the radiant warmth of My life as all about you are cries of pain. It is to this pain that the love you share with Me brings answers, but not as you know answers in the world.

My answers abound in you but you are afraid of our dialogue because you think you have betrayed your higher self. Come nevertheless, it will expand your heart until the time when all resistance is gone from you. You will hear the quiet knowing, you will know yourself.

You are all that I am. Be assured of this. There is nothing separating us. Trust your imagination. It will make Me real to you. ✧

ANGEL III

✦

As muted shadows crisscross the meadow covered in moonlight, a story is being told by the markings left upon it. You read there the story of your life from Before and Beyond and Forever. A story altogether more wonderful than what you remember a life could be.

You live in a subtle reality that tells your story wherever you look. You are a light that brings forth what is believed hidden. But there is nothing hidden. From the inner world wrapped in oblivion you are forever calling forth invisibleness into form and expression. Oh how tender is the soft light of your soul mirrored in the soft morning light of your Earthly home.

You are the delicate child of a gossamer One so strong in Its nothingness. You are held in patient arms. You are embodied for quiet and confident expression and your day will confirm this. You unfold as a gently turning wheel needing no destination but the beauty of its self-expression. ✧

ANGEL IV

✦

Freedom is a reality bigger than the world. It opens the vista of living. It brings the soft, kind wind of imagination to move all things in the direction they want to go. It is life.

It is your life. It stands underneath you, supporting you in the most complete way. It is the song the Thrush in your heart sings to wake you in the morning. It is the unfurling of your limbs that permits you to climb the highest mountain as if propelled by wings of mightiness. Freedom has come with you into the dream. It is by your side and under-girds you, protecting you from all confusion of spirit and mind. It is your own true self. ✧

ANGEL V

✦

Spirals of feelings are making sounds only the one who listens can hear. You are the listener of thoughts not thought in a world unaware of a loveliness that comes from a heart that says nothing loud.

Yours is the heart that offers the stars to the night of the sun. Yours is the footstep on the smooth sands upon which the living waters ebb and flow. The Reality that never goes away is walking with you as you search for this thing that is your self.

No one has been misplaced. ✧

ANGEL VI

✦

You are not on a path to completion, you are complete. You are not inventing, you are discovering. You are not free-floating somewhere 'out there' needing to accomplish anything with your life. You reveal the life that is.

Why are you feeling lost? Because you are not feeling found. You are found, and have only acquired a *feeling* of loss. What you have is a belief that something strange happened to you and that you had to obey and agree with it. You are waiting for this to be resolved before you can act. But there is no waiting in life. Life is the Flow of substance that has no beginning and no end. You are where you are meant to be. Use your imagination to remain out of the false perception of the world. ✧

ANGEL VII

✦

There pours out of you a Silent River—deep and full
with love. It carries the Light from which all lights shine and
every star twinkles. It flows from the Source of all and holds
all expressions of Itself in the tenderest care; in the most
cherishing arms.

None will fall. None will bring forth what is not. It is
one breath that is breathed in all of expressive form. It is
the beginning that had no start and will not end. It is the
strength that murmurs softness. It is the stillness that is full
of song. It is this one and that one and the other one within
the only One.

You know this. ✧

ANGEL VIII

✦

You are a being filled with a splendor that seeks to bring Itself forth as you. You are the recipient of this givingness you have to give. Sit and wait in happy attendance to your true self and then bring it to the days and nights that cannot shine until you do. In the Earth-world you have been asked to look away from the activity of life that flows from within outwards. You have locked yourself out of the power of true movement. And so you run after what is never needed and value form over qualities of mind and heart.

Your accumulations will not last—they are wisps of thought. You stand far from the peace of this moment, far from what is eternal. You no longer believe such a place exists.

But it does. ✧

ANGEL IX

✦

You have lost nothing of My tender nature. You will find it when you look beyond the form of outer experience. The "peace that passeth understanding," is not comprehended by human thinking.

Do not stare at what appears real. Look within and contemplate the presence of what cannot be told. There am I for I cannot be found anywhere else. Be soft, be released of effort. See what cannot be found in the glitter of a world enamored of shiny things. It is easy, you can do this. You are this. Do not wait for others to join you. Stand seemingly alone in good company with yourself and know that the dearest name is your own.

Soften your quest for wisdom. It is not something to strive for. It already exists. Accept without outer proof that Life is at hand undergirding and supporting your being and blessing your human world as I guide you in all your ways. Stand firm and steady on inner contemplation; it takes nothing more than this to be with Me. Be still, dear one. Be still and know that this moment is full with Life. ✧

ANGEL X

✦

Trust in the words that are now coming from your heart.
The words I speak to you are understood by the deepest
part of you. You see all about you your neighbors pursuing
only outer achievements. They appear so convinced, so
determined, so unconflicted in the things they think are
needed. You do not do as they do, but in subtle ways you
are influenced. It is the way of the human mind to be
influenced, and so you doubt yourself. You are not enough in
touch with the wisdom that has never left you, the wisdom
that keeps you unperturbed by the world of human events.

Come to the quiet moment between us and hear the
reassurance I bring. Your loyalty must be to yourself. Loyalty
to anything else has occurred but from poor management of
your thoughts, and for no other reason. The world doesn't
need your love, it needs *Love*. I give it through you, when
you are at peace with yourself. ✧

ANGEL XI

✦

Your eyes. They give you trouble. But you know your eyes are not in danger. You do not see with your eyes. You see with your understanding. And you think you have lost your understanding.

You have lost nothing. You are not the world that is a mere distortion of what is. You are the world that is peaceful and made of beauty. You can look through distortion and see beauty. It is a simple thing to do. Your eyes are not eyes designed for distortion; your eyes are the means the light flows outwardly to show the qualities of the light within you.

You have been so sad thinking you see an unhappy world. You have been disappointed in yourself for thinking you are creating an unhappy world. Do not use your eyes to deceive yourself. Use your eyes to let Me show you the world I see. Believe in yourself, there is nothing else to believe in. ✧

ANGEL XII

✦

Your innocence is vast in Me. It brightens the very being of Being. You are the Light that never can be diminished and this Light carries you through the pathway of sleep that is your human dream. Even as you dream, your uniqueness is Me and all that is Mine. You are the impulses within peace. Nothing is too grand for you to contemplate. Nothing is too wonderful to trust and have. You have not needed to draw the darkness over your elation at being alive. You have not had to compromise the Joy that is your nature, for you have but one nature and it is eternally joyful.

You can trust the desires from your soul and be indifferent to how many do not share this vision with you. Give to yourself all that I am in you. You have been lonely without It.

Let yourself feel the exuberance that I breathe into you. Let its presence in your inner mind not confuse you in the dreaming world. They are not in conflict. One is the real, the other, not. Let the Light shine through your temple self and come *from* Me *from* Me *from* Me. Be whole as only I can make wholeness. ✧

ANGEL XIII

✦

We meet again. We will always meet, but not in this manner—you are bringing yourself from within a slumber.

We meet to remind you we never parted. And for you to be assured that all is well with you—a wellness that extends to your human world. All things are in their proper place and your heart nursed from harmony and joy.

You begin to glimpse that one single step is needed. Just the smallest impulse to walk towards Me and I do the rest. You see how simple it is to know Me. I am at the center of all that concerns you. I am the circumference of all that fulfills you, I build your worlds and moments. You needn't effort, only choose. A glimpse inward, a nod to My Presence, and the day's burdens fall off your shoulders. So quiet is the true world. So soft is the Eternal Reality. So dear is the love that is your nature. You are the child who lives in oneness and never grew up to believe in a world of mere survival. Stop looking with such earnestness at the world of mere survival. ✧

ANGEL XIV

✦

You are often so weary. Constantly thinking, looking, hearing, seeing, touching, absorbing mere concepts, is not good for you. You want to stop the world that drowns out your equanimity.

Can you look beyond the world made by *this* human mind, and *that* human mind, and *your* human mind? It is permissible to ignore so intense a world.

You forget to tell yourself you are spinning to a waltz of mirages, even benign ones, in an enchanted ballroom built from eccentric thoughts and manners, charming as they often are. You need respite from this *outerness*—urged from *within*, you will thrive without effort.

What is disruptive about the thoughts and manners of this human world, as charming as they often are, is that they weigh you down with lies about yourself. To incessantly hear what is *not true* is tiring. ✧

ANGEL XV

✦

You have been proud of your ability to sacrifice, to compromise. You have taken it as a sign of intelligence and courage. You admire your levelheadedness, your pragmatism. You admired these traits and chose them every time over something that you thought frivolous. It is My quiet nature that you thought frivolous. Being gentle was not important—not supported by the culture, not "real life."

Your nature is gentle. The only thing that you know and ever express when you let yourself not think about it, is gentleness. Come, make peace with frivolity. You have a lovely tale to tell yourself and others. ✧

It matters not what you do in the world. It matters not
what you have said and to whom. It matters not any of it.
What matters, is that you turn your attention inward and
believe that your life is here in the splendor so clear to your
heart. It will be manifested for you as a world of peace and
goodness. You bless more than yourself when you touch
your true being.

Believe in the wonders of Wonder. Your inner stillness has
tales to tell. Your inner stillness has truths to reveal. Your
inner stillness is your right place in the human world. Be still
and know you are home and are living from the Light that
lights the world. ✧

ANGEL XVII

✦

Is there power in a *loving poetic* sigh?

Can something so slight, so delicate, so gentle, so contrary to the psychological constructs of a human being be the cause and support of all life?

This invisible reality, so easy to forget in a sensual world, is the one you remember coming from.

Remember now. ✧

ANGEL XVIII

✦

How good is the day that belongs to Me and not to the
world. How good is the day that placidly accepts your
touch. In your touch is the substance you possess to make
a good earth. There is wonder in you that is needed in the
world. You come bringing images and wordings that you did
not at first perceive as images and wordings because they
lived unformed in you as a warmth, a quiet knowing,
a deeply felt stirring.

All this stirring caused a desire in you to share, to let be
known, to tell, to assure, to reassure. And now you are.
It is not the days of denial and separation that mark your
journey on Earth. No, it is the presence of the Presence
within you that became the gifts of your expression. These
honor your life. Giving them honors Me. You waded through
the confusion, the misunderstanding, the glazed eyes, the
censorship. You persevered. Take pleasure in offering your
gifts into expression. Rejoice in the goodness your life
conveys. You are your own reward. ✧

ANGEL XIX

✦

You have lived a whole human life to arrive at your understanding. You built your peace with self while in a world asleep to all that is true of love.

You came to this world to transform your mind, to clear your path of mental encumbrances. You have done this to expand your authoritative countenance with eternity. You have brought the truth to the contrary thoughts that made you see a dream of separation. Now you can be in this world and see joy and goodness. You can be here and . . . shine The Light!

It is done. Amen. ✧

WHEN ALL IS SAID AND DONE

It Was Only a Dream

I WAITED FOR MY SELF, SO PATIENTLY

✦

FROM THE CREST OF THE HILL I see her. A small figure, she has a face I cannot quite make out. She stands immobile and seems to be waiting. I am intrigued because her waiting has a loveliness about it. It is not an empty waiting but one filled with peace, so very different from my own. As I watch her I vaguely wonder what has happened to my usual awareness.

I walk in her direction. My movements are tentative and slow until I notice the path reaching to hold my steps. Nothing has taken place but this sweet unexpected thing and somehow I am different. Something has been restored to me.

At the end of the path where she stands, she is holding a little candle. As I walk I know the path is leading us to one another. I will not lose my way. The candle's flame shimmers and appears to reach for me. The candle's light is pure awareness. The candle's light is the world. I understand this.

As I walk, I feel I am walking on air. No. The air is walking me. I do not stop to ponder this as I recognize that the one I go to is waiting from a sense of our not being apart. She stands in such tranquility that something calm takes over my mind and makes me peaceful without any thought of how it is occurring. Have I laid down my burdens?

She smiles now as if in answer. It is a small smile, as discreet as the countenance that brings it forth. I've missed this quiet regard from life, having witnessed little of it in my world.

I am walking under a night sky filled with glitter. I see that she stands by a lovely garden and I can feel it welcome me. I like the thought of a garden with friendly beckoning ways. I like knowing a garden can do this. I remember a receptive universe where I was welcome in all its many rooms.

I sense I need do nothing to alter myself to join with this garden. It is What Is. I am What Is. I feel seams that held me bound loosen and fall away. They go nowhere, I soon see that they never existed. Along with these odd bits of binding go the thoughts and feelings that have kept me bowed low in that world with a purpose not my own.

I am close now to the quiet one who has remained standing so steadily. She is soft of demeanor and without sound. She is kind and I know she is constant. I am not sure how I know, but I do. In her presence doubt is not a possibility.

I am now deeply conscious of this path I walk on and I want to stay in this serene world and enter that garden. I take a breath. The path has become brighter as if within it lives the dawn. It is a dawn so deep and pure that it does not announce itself by any means other than by being.

With my next step I feel something old move away. What was important a moment ago is not important now. Reality is replacing itself with Itself. Reality is moving me into another incarnation of myself. It is beautiful to walk this path.

Suddenly, in a very soft way, life has become uncomplicated. I am uninvolved in saving my life. Suddenly, there is no urgency to . . . anything. Suddenly, I see all things as they truly are. I am what I am meant to be—fulfilled from simplicity. I am unconcerned with the list of scribbles on the chalkboard always staring back at me.

I hear the quiet—its voice is spine-tingling, its language soothing. It is a presence that fills all and everything and forever. It is more real than night and day. *I am your self*, it says from nowhere but everywhere.

But I am unhurried to know more. This moment is sufficient. I hear something else in the silence, *Be unhurried, gentle soul, child of Infinity. Be calm and trusting for there is no forgetting. You are the love that never went away. There is no other life.*

I am standing before the garden now and find my hands are holding a little candle. I know I am about to enter the home of my sacred self. This is the place my heart never left; the place that has given me the trees and the sun of my human world to keep me from missing too much the world that lives within me.

Surprisingly, I am hesitant to enter the garden. The thought that I am writing all this into a book a sleeping world will read disturbs me. Can I write about what is not believed there? All of my human life I never let myself be what others couldn't perceive.

In the timelessness of things as I write this, I know someone is reading what I am writing. But I know something else, too. I know that the one reading has asked for this journey and is joyfully welcomed on this path and into this garden. The inner world is more than mine, it is ours. What I give to myself becomes that world—the world contained in a single candle flame.

✦

I am writing this while you are reading this. Somewhere beyond where we think we are writer and reader, we are something deep and wonderful. And one. This truth transforms our human world. ✧

THE BEST STORY FOR LAST

I was in the middle of washing the dishes, when something within me made me turn to my little dog and say: "Mimi, I'm going to write a poem." And with that, I dried my hands, found my pen and notebook, and wrote a poem.

I turned it into a "children's" book. Over the years it acquired many incarnations as the artwork evolved and deepened and I found my way to tell the story of our imagination and its powerful law.

Now, a long time later, this story has found its place at the end of this book. After all, there are no grown-ups among us. ✧

A TALE OF HOW THE
UNIVERSE BEGAN

We have come on Earth to play at make-believe but ponder if you will the treasures hidden up your sleeve.

Let me tell you a tale of never growing old and of the Silence where your innocence is told.

It's a bold and daring remembrance of all the things you are, for in the inner reaches of yourself, you are the *Light* within the star.

This story is yours and mine and you will see we two entwine an act of sun where we become a One.

✦

Now, spread your thoughts as you would wings and delight in the merry-madness this contemplation brings . . .

Long, long ago,

but really *just now*,

a deep Vastness

stood beautiful

and still

and invisible.

Its name: FOREVER.

Cosmic Universe

of electric emotion,

loving all of Itself.

And *before* we came to be

loving you and me and us and Tree.

So it was.

One.

Loving.

Loving so true

and loving so long

that in the urge to love

it became a *bud*

that its gentle face be known.

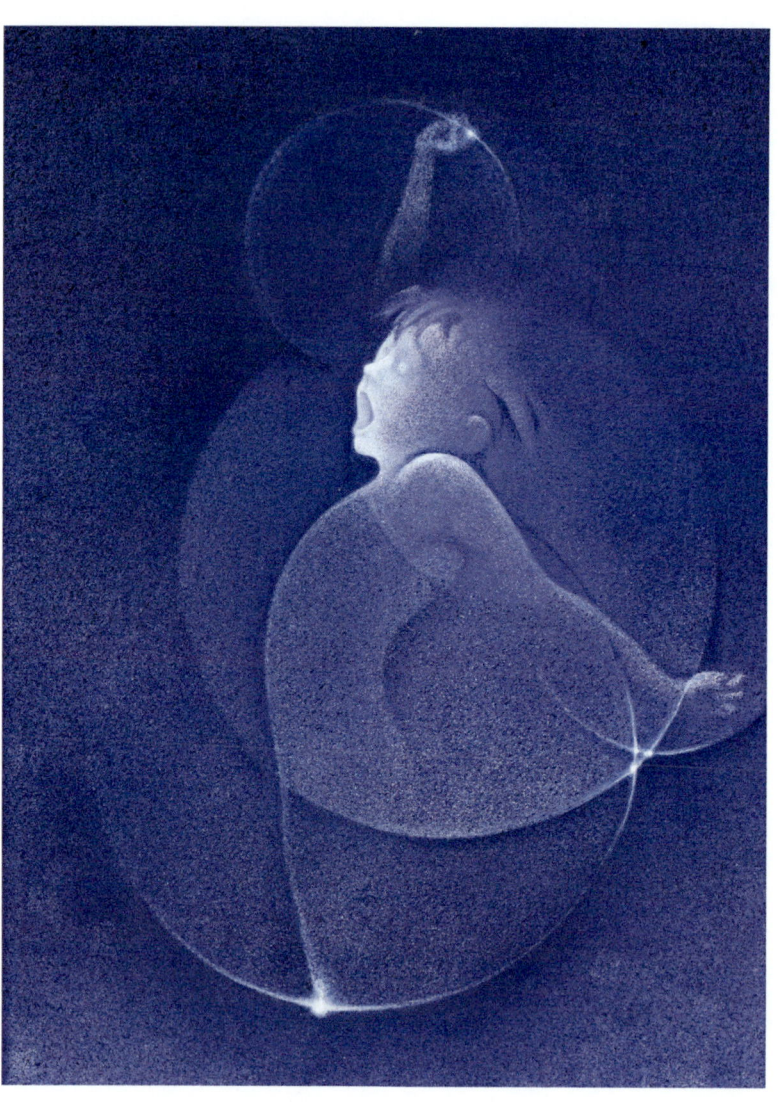

The throbbing from this Heart
so giving
filled the Vastness-of-It-All
to become
something living.

The bud stirred
and moved
and drew a breath.
Then from *within* itself
it knew. . .
"I AM," it said.
And was.

"I AM LIGHT," it said,
and turned the night into day.
"I AM BRIGHT," it said,
as the colors showed
an exuberant and
harmonious Form!

Alone
throughout the heavens
the little bud sang and played
until, the thoughtful moment,
it stopped itself to say,
"Surely, I am more than myself."

And lo and behold,
in the twist of a tracing
there was *another* self
it found itself facing!

"OH, I AM A *WE!*"
the little bud cried.
And in an instant
all his loneliness died.

"I am a WE!" he shouted with glee.
"We are a we!"
"We are."
"We are."

A he and a she.
Two voices lifted
into *one* lovely song —
the sound getting louder,
the ring getting strong . . .

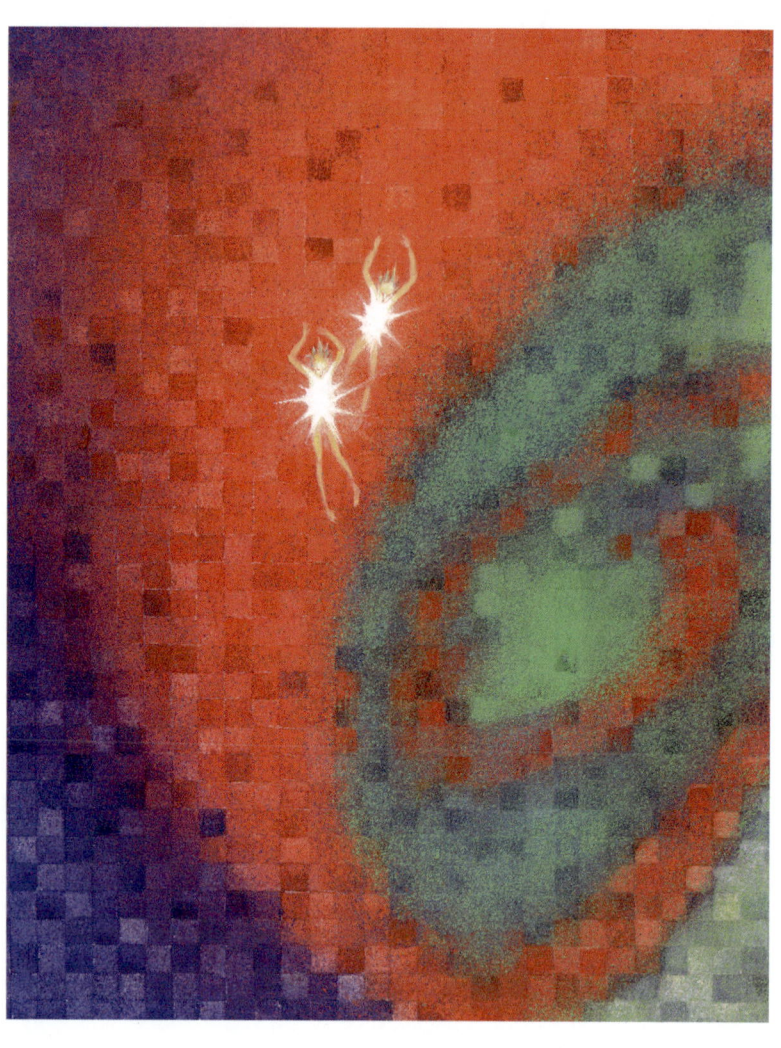

All heaven was moved
to a rush of vibration
converging and merging
in rich syncopation.

It swirled and whirled
and began to expand

until

in the sigh of a moment
it stopped,
as if soothed by a hand.

And in the instant that is

right now

THE WORLDS BEGAN

✦

So. This is the tale. It is all true.

There is magic in living and power in you.

You are what life's made of and this

is your story.

You're the image of love—your word

is your glory,

And when you bring something new into

being—sing out with your heart,

I AM *what I'm seeing.*

Que bella

magnifico

The Beginning. . .

ARLENE GRASTON was born in Reims, France, to an American father and French mother, and enjoys a dual nationality. She began her career apprenticing with the haute couture house of Nina Ricci in Paris, for whom she also designed jewelry.

In her twenties Arlene came to New York and established her own graphic design studio. Her commercial work appeared in national publications and on Broadway with posters for the original Broadway productions of BUBBLING BROWN SUGAR and EUBIE!. Despite her success in the commercial world, Arlene, an entirely self-taught artist, chose eventually to express only the spiritual images that have always lived within her. From earliest childhood, her human experience has been informed by her conscious awareness of life before birth. She dedicates her work as an artist to the Wonder that is the reality of Life. It needs to be believed in for happiness.

Her art has been exhibited in New York and London. She lives with her husband in New York City. She may be contacted through her website: *arlenegraston.com.*

ABOUT THE ART

All the original art in this book was hand-painted in gouache on Strathmore 500 Series Bristol. Gouache is an opaque water-based natural pigment paint with a warm, velvet finish enabling subtle brushwork. The actual paintings average 16 x 20 inches. Arlene's body of work can be seen on *nyvisibles.com.*

37891692R00082

Made in the USA
Columbia, SC
01 December 2018